If
GOD
Could
RAP

(Rhythm & Poetry)

Written By

HAFIS

Copyright © 2022
Author: Hafis
Mount Vernon NY 10550
ISBN : 979-8-218-05808-1
Printed in the United States

This book is dedicated first to my mother and father

Dolores Williams & Alonzo Gordon

I thank the Most high Adonai for the gifts

My family and friends (UTLM), those who supported me along the way

And my Moorish brothers in the Moorish Science Temple #10

And, around the world......

Table of Contents
Foreword by K'wan

Introduction

DM ENTANGLEMENT

KILLUMANITI

PRISON INDUSTRIAL COMPLEX

NAKED

NO FOOD

GOLD MIND

TYPE OF TIME

REAL NEGUS

BLACK PANTHER

SHE LIKE RAPPERS

NEGUS 2 GODS

RAP/HIP HOP EXORCISM

POLYGYNY

FRIENEMIES

WE DON'T

ROLE MODEL

FOREWORD BY KWAN

IF GOD COULD RAP:

"If God had a name, what would it be? And would you call it to His face if you were faced with Him? In all His glory, what would you ask of Him? If you had just one question, what would you ask of Him? What if God was one of us?" - Joan Osborne

When I first discovered that song, "One of Us," I listened to it a lot. It would often drive people crazy who had the misfortune of riding in a car with me, and I was controlling the radio. No one could quite understand what I found so fascinating about this folksy white woman crooning about God riding on a bus. What very few were able to grasp was that it wasn't about the song but the line of thinking which inspired it. What if God was one of us?

9

What if this entity that we were raised seeing depicted as a grand celestial being, who hovers in the skies above us, passing judgment on the wicked and the good alike, wasn't spirit at all but simply a man? Or woman, depending? What if the prayers that we send to heaven didn't have quite that far to travel because God was as close as your next-door neighbor or the bus driver you see every morning while you're riding to work or school? To the casual listener, this song revolves around a question, but if you listen a little deeper, you'll discover that Joan was making an observation.

People look to God for strength, love, clarity... When we pray, the prayer is usually asking God to tap into something that's already inside of us and make it greater. God, teach me how to be a better lover. God, help me to get through this storm. God, help me to tap into that part of me that I don't have the strength to reach on my own. God, I am the clay for you to sculpt as you see fit. God's blessings come from the raw material we give Him to work with. So, is God not already in us all? Don't answer that yet. Read the rest of the forward and then revisit this part.

When my cousin, Hafis, first confided in me that he was writing a book, I immediately assumed it would be based on an account of his life. I mean, why wouldn't it? If you know my cousin, you understand that his road to where he is now was anything but the traditional one. From early in life, the universe had made it clear that his life would not be an easy one. There have been highs, lows, setbacks, and get-backs. So why wouldn't this story be the first one fired from his chamber? And then he showed me how deep the rabbit hole went, and I understood.

In Hafis, I present a man who was dropped into less than favorable conditions and adapted. A man who has suffered losses and continued on. A man who had questions of faith and found his own answers. There have been many phases during the transformation from Demetrius, to Danger and finally Hafis. The constant through all of these changes was his love for music. It was the music in which he found his raw material for God to work with. And in the music, the God in him is reflected.

So as to the question, "What if God was one of us?" I reply, God is all of us.

INTRODUCTION

RAP. The first thing you will learn from this book is that the word RAP in the music genre means "Rhythm and Poetry." Today, in its full capacity, it's a lost art form. In a world of legendary urban street poets and great rappers like NAS, DMX, Notorious B.I.G., Jay-Z, and 2Pac. Lyrics in Rap/Hip Hop songs in mainstream media today have been dumbed down to pure ignorance, negative vibrational perceptional self-talk, and mumbo jumbo. One has to ask themselves whether this is the evolution of the genre or on purpose. Purposely done to program the minds of the youth? The power of words is as true as water is wet. Words cast spells for those who bear witness to the magic in speech. Unlike Rap/Hip Hop in the past, we had a balance with rap groups like Public Enemy, A Tribe Called Quest, and X-Clan to the street ballots of the '90s with Mobb Deep, CNN, Snoop Dogg, and Wu-Tang Clan. Most of today's rap lyrics lack substance, influential positive energy, and sustenance for the listener. This does the listener a great injustice and robs them of the power of words. When in the beginning, there was only the word, and the word was with the GODs.

What makes up a true rap song is rhythm and poetry. A marriage that cannot be denied as perfect matrimony. Rap as an art form must be balanced with these two ingredients for it to truly be a RAP song by definition. This book is unique, one of its first kind. Poetry of this urban magnitude hasn't been published like this before. It highlights the importance of rap lyrics having meaning. Conveying a message to teach, reach, or repel any person, place, experience, or idea in the listener's mind. I'm a Sufi Moor by birth and faith, a professional rap performing artist, writer, speaker, entrepreneur, and actor.

Everything in the universe is vibrations and frequency. When we sing, talk, or even whisper, our vocal cords vibrate at different frequencies. These frequencies and vibrations can set the tone for a person, a room, bar, or concert hall and affect the vibe or the situation's outcome. What we speak, we draw to ourselves. Therefore the saying goes, "Watch what you say" and "Be careful of what you ask for." The English language alone is covertly composed of words that negatively trap us daily, drawing energies to ourselves. All while unbeknownst to the speaker or listener. But that's another book altogether— Be on the lookout!

You, obviously, are one to appreciate words if you are reading this far into the introduction. No matter your sex, where you're from, race, creed, or culture. We know words do matter. Lyrics have transformed my life personally at times when I needed comfort, understanding of what I was going through at that time, and sometimes even just a good distraction from the troubles of the world. We dance, laugh, and cry to the songs that sing to our hearts. I grew up back in the concrete jungle of New York City. We utilized music to help us get through the struggle and pain.

Rap music told our story as young copper-colored children. We mimicked them and recited the lyrics to the songs as if we had written them ourselves. Those songs we remember all our lives. Some songs spark emotions from that time; others bring back glimpses of good and bad memories. These songs transformed our lives consciously and subconsciously. The beat moved you while the words in the lyrics fed you the MC's perspective and POV. The difference between now and then is making sense of what is being said. RAP has always told the story of the have-nots, the oppressed, and the downtrodden. The poems in this book are no different. They tell the true story of every one of us who has experienced the context of the poems in this book. And even if you haven't, after reading this book, you will have felt like you have.

These poems will resonate with those who can relate, but on the flip side, it will help those who are not from this culture or demographic to understand more about the inner city, the youth and what we go through in the struggle to survive poverty, crime-riddled neighborhoods and low-class social treatments perpetuated by a long history of racism. I wrote them in my time of despair, pain, love, contemplation, and discontentment. My divine form of expression. Many of them were written during my transition from unconscious to conscious, sleep to awaken, from a hardcore hip hop rapper, then back to a Sufi Moor.

While some of you may beg to differ because of the vulgarity, these poems were divinely inspired. Because from my point of view, all is GOD inspired whether we want to give her credit or not. Nothing can exist without God; she is the sustainer of all things, even divine inspirations. All art, whether you consider it bad or good, is the expression of one's spirit and the spirit is one with source, the universe, or whatever you recognize as the true living force in your life. Notice I said, "Her." Yeah, I'll do that sometimes as a writer. Make you go, Hmmm... But again, that's a whole other book altogether— be on the lookout!

If GOD Could RAP is my life story inspired by a rhythm and my thoughts. If GOD lived my life, which is a misnomer, He most certainly would RAP about the same topics and social ills of this poetry book. Big facts!

My truth is GOD lives in me, around me, and through me. From my experiences, my spirit evolved like the caterpillar, and this book is the butterfly. May these poems created from song lyrics, give the reader what they are missing in RAP music today. The power of words. Hearing the words to a song has a totally different effect than reading the words to a song.

These poems are meant for you to read with an open mind but it may not be for the narrow-minded, bougie, faint and/or, in some cases, parental discretion may be advised.

ALIF (GOD) ON MY SIDE

Why is this world against me?

This life of white supremacy

The Moorish man's the enemy

When really we all energy

Why do you have people thinking my skin is evil?

Who is inferior?

If God created us all equal

Why are police and SECRET SOCIETIES all against me?

What's the big secret you think you hold against me?

The Maafa of Hiram Abiff

But I have risen

No more suffering; this is for the ghetto, Moorish children

We on the verge of spiritual revolution, it's evolution

People are waking up to the bullshit y'all doing

And I know I risk persecution, but I have no fear because death is but an illusion

I'm one with light, and light is everywhere

MAGNUM OPUS

This is my magnum opus

I don't know who to trust

Money ain't enough, guns ain't enough

My ancient Kemetic high in a Kush state of mind

Cheikh Ahmadou Bamba said it's all by design

The food you deprive

Make the hungry commit crimes

Then you put us in prison

This shit's by design

So, I'm going to use this vibe to liberate minds

As within, so without, the plan is divine

Who lacks spiritual comprehension won't take what I'm giving

So, just go to the next poem; regardless, I'm winning

Machine nation of a hidden nation

I'm just saying you got to use your intuition

How come the Supreme Court hasn't overturned the Dred Scott decision?

ASHÉ

Said her name was Ashé

Moon magic

Met her on a Monday

By Friday, she was my Oshun

No towel, dripping water in my bedroom

Where Mars rules and stars bloom

Moving fast

Ferrari gives her leg room

When the streets stress me out, I call you

I just want to love you,

"Ashé!"

At the crossroad, Eshu sent you

I'm in the streets trying to keep my cup full

'Cause ain't no mercy in the streets when the strap pull

Oh! Ashé, Ashé, Ashé!!!

Big butt cellulite, she got big dreams

Eshu, and I don't want no issues

No drama, she don't want a real nigga

She wants a God-king whose vision's bigger
on her team; she has big dreams!

GOLD DIGGER

First comes the music, then comes the money

After that, the Gold Diggers

They ain't getting nothing from me

Eye got nothing for them

but

Nut and honey,

Nothing, honey!

Here, take a taste of this Nut & Honey

Sweet like Ben & Jerry's

Hard like Halle Berry

Taste strawberries when I'm cutting it
missionary

Stronger than straight Henny

Your Mr. Goodbar

Good & Plenty...

I go deeper than the code of Da Vinci

Asking her, "Do you feel me the deeper I go?"

But she only answers

With a moan & groan

I make her shake it fast, like when Mystikal was home

DA MESSAGE

A mother's water burst

She about to have a seed; they got plans for it

It's a conspiracy

Now, let's guess, what will he grow to be?

A baller, lawyer, or an MC?

Or maybe just a bum living on the street

Or crazy in a prison infirmary

They got us under pressure

My generation's X

Where do we turn next?

Is it to that dresser to get the Chrome Tech

And go berserk, no matter how hard we work

We make lesser

Got to stoop to lower measures to live better

So, his pleasure becomes sex, money, and guns

Benz interior plum, jewelry weighing a ton

Like his ancestors, the people God blesses

The oppresses distresses

Sending out S.O.S's for their stresses

G's PARADISE

A Gangsta pays a price

Looking for paradise

But ain't no paradise

Under the city lights

Up on the late-night, chasing a paradise

We looking outside when it's inside

We all running wild, looking for paradise

But ain't no paradise

Under the city lights

A Gangsta's paradise is in his heart and eyes

Follow Deme Melody, homie

I'll show you to the light

BY DESIGN

The only way he thinks he can make it

Is if he takes it

They knew he would sell crack

And start to chase it

Through the rat holes of every city

Like the Matrix

Vicious gun fights

Giving each other facelifts

They knew we would do what we all do

Kill me, kill you

It's all political; I'm Red, I'm Blue

It's pitiful

These young Negus aren't scared of you or the ridicule

They pity the fool with the rustiest tool

Revelations, The Coming

Negus, trust me, it's soon

All my young G's

Just stay tuned, roll with us or move, win with us or lose!

We'll lead the greatest spiritual takeover under the moon

FREEDOM

My mother told me life is priceless

Sought a hell with the usual slight twist

What happened to all the Assata's and Isis?

Young M.C.'s, you have my permission to bite this

Strange to me taught to bang since three

All the people running around claiming they free

To do as they please

But when they ask for human rights

How come they say, "Please"?

And got to petition

While baby girl tired of stripping

Hoping a man provides a better living

Listen! You don't have to like this

Because that's not why I write this

There's a war going on; I'm trying to fight this

Negative, danger official down to the bone gristle

Splitting these demons with my semen and nickel pistols

If you had to fight for your freedom

Would you?

HATER IN DENIAL

Even with this talent, I'm still struggling

Hugging my fake friends

Trying to figure out will all the hate end

The younger generation scramble for bacon

A mother's world is shaken

When her only child's life was taken

I'm thinking about retaliating

But it won't never end

They hit me; I hit them

We hit each other and leave our women here to suffer

I called her a Bitch

But she know that I love her

Covered in wickedness

Not crying wolf, we all witness this

Our babies inherit sickness instead of the riches

No money, just guns, saying, "Daddy used to
grip this."

Snitches are breeding snitches

Thugs are breeding thugs

But where is the love at?

There is none, from what I'm seeing

So, if you breathing jealousy, smell your breath

And if you living like a snake, sleep with your
vest

BREAK GENERATIONAL CURSES

My homie incarcerated forever & tries to raise
his bad kids through letters

It can't get any worse but it's not getting no
better

A Beretta could feed a family or hurt plenty

Single mothers work hard and try to save every
penny

A message to the melanin woman

Don't you see what they are doing to me?

Divide us so we can't breed...

What I need

Is your support

I know I did you wrong, but this is how I was
taught

Fought to hold my chin up

Wondering where will I end up

One in the neck in my Lex coup bent up

The landlord is a coward; he raised the rent up

I apologize, not providing a male source

But now I know

I behold of a pale horse

Putting powder on the scale or attending Yale, boss

You still a Nigga

Crossing enemy lines in these envious times

Thuggin' through the struggling

INCARCERATED SISTARS

Sistar, never worry & stay in the law library

I gave my mom a little something for your commissary

Your sons are innocent

Struggle is hereditary

So, when the nights might get alone and
scary

I would tell them to listen to Makaveli Hail
Mary

And pray for they mommy

And call Keisha when they can't find me

I'm on the road to take care of the family

So we can give these seeds what they need
to succeed

When I speak, they can't deny me

Cousins, but because of Crack/Cocaine, we
became brother & sister

Grew up in grandma's house as brother and
sister

Look how drugs and disease affect us, sister

It all goes back to another poem, The System

A cycle made to keep us in the system

This is for you, my sister in the system

SYSTEM

This one goes out to all my brothers in the system

But can't forget my sisters in the system

Whatever happened to the sisters in the system?

We hardly mention the sisters in the system

Dealt the same hand as brothers in the system

I know firsthand

My sister's in the system

Eye see her face in her kids when I kiss 'em

Sis, don't cry, Eye know you really miss them

Doing your time in federal women's prison

Eye feel your pain; you know eye was in the system

Coxsackie, Bedford Hills, the same system

It's all entrapment they got us all locked up in

Read scripture so you can understand the system, so you can overcome and over-stand the system

You know I love you and I miss you, so I had to cough this pain up out of my system

BLACK IS A COLOR, NOT A RACE

Playing Chess where the black piece moves first

Shooting pool with an all-black cue

Last ball you have to knock off is white, or you lose

All black world, All black state

Statue of Liberty with an all-black face

Black bezel, my nizzle just caught a case

Conspiracy trying to be the black Bill Gates

All black jail, black mail when he write

Where the prison population is 90% white

Black iPads, DEMEGOD playlist

Black Hollywood

Where the A-list the black list?

It's like Prince Hall in a black house

I'm a blacksmith when I pull that hammer out

My black Goddess yoni is like the black hole

I get behind them and give them the black
Mamba

That black anaconda

That's that black Power

DRIP MELANIN

Drip melanin, Drip melanin

Two stepping with my weapon and Fez

Look how canary ice drip off my melanin

She a baddie with a phatty

Dripping melanin

Tell them I want my models all dark-skinned

From the car to the bar

We dripping melanin

Every girl in the world wants melanin

These dudes are day room; I don't know
what to say to them

It's over, haters' sick, Corona

I just want to grip because I want to drip

The virus got these zombies on some death
wish

My bruja a shooter and a good witch

I told her cast a spell on the hood snitch

Cook up some bad luck

On him and his bad bitch

Black girl magic

It's the Moorish drip

Try to G check my shit, bet I get it lit

BLACK-A-MOOR

Black Jesus in a black robe

Like a black Pope in the Catacombs

Under the city of black Rome

Black Mass

Worshiping a Black calf

Priest take offerings

Thieves in black masks

Black nuns twerking in a Black church

The Black Madonna, with a black Birkin purse

A Black honeymoon on a beach with black sand

One set of footprints as we walk, holding hands

Pitch black room, I make her say my name

Hot Black sex like the Chronicles of Zane

When l bust

She's impregnated with the pain

Love making, creating black magic

Nails painted black, digging in my back

Nine months later, she in labor with the work

Pull up at the hospital in an all-black hearse

BLACK PHALLUS

Every girl in the world welcome to my palace

They come from afar to pay homage to the phallus

DEME stay fly

I don't need no stylist

Baby girl took a bow, vowed to be of service

Take off your Jimmy Choo's

No shoes in the house of worship

She like the club Mile High & the Egyptian
Ba

I'm between her wings, getting head in the
sky

To my Black Goddess,

I promise to keep it honest

She know when I'm excited, it's Washington Monument

She want to kiss the Washington Monument

So, I let her put her lips to the Obelisk

Her true religion is money & phallicism

So, I had to ask her,

"What if GOD was a rapper? Would you make love to Him in the Aston Martin faster?"

If He took you to His temple in Calabasas

She want to get poppin' like a molly and two Cialis

I got her on her knees like she praying

DM ENTANGLEMENT

The yoni got him sprung, coughing up a lung

Screaming, "DEME,

Stay out my B.M. DM!"

No, I don't know her, and I never met her

But on the low,

Me and her know better

Small waist, pretty face with the bubble

I tell her man whatever to keep her out of
trouble

Because she got that water

I think I love her

Poland Spring and her squirt game mean

Drip queen, drip queen

Tell him you going to karaoke

You like to lip-synch any song featuring the
God-King

She know she wrong and want to do the
right thing

It's in her eyes; I can see it in her eyes

He make her mad and then buy her a bag

True lies

She tired of being tired

His time has expired

Your man not on his job

Tell him that he's fired

Looking for a reason, going through your DM

And that's when he sees them

I'm all up in them

Thread deep, I'm all up in them

She a freak, so I'm all up in them

Killumaniti

While New York and California is under water

From earthquakes, high tides rise over four corners

This will bump via satellite

At high performance

As the end comes up on us

Remember this verse

Mama said always put God first

Remember, the devil is alive, walking the earth

He can be your enemy or closest friend

I nodded my head yes and hit the streets again

New York, N.Y.

Let's take it back to the source

I got a full-course meal to get you a mill

There are a few sell outs that need to be killed

Moved out the hood, and they not giving back

Go and see them negus and I will see you when you get back

Best believe that

Negus, you know I'm going to bless you

The spook who sat by the window of the coup

In my hood

It's hard enough to deal with the police asses

So, I be damned if I take shit from racist activist

The newest edition to Hip Hop's kitchen

One of the main ingredients that's missing

SNITCHING IN HEAVEN

Now, if I go to heaven and you go to hell

You rat-ass negus probably tell

Yell my government name on some Sammy
the Bull shit

Have GOD send me back to the fiery pit

Because the fire I write is worth a thousand
sins

To the bangers on Rikers Island getting it in,
or the wolves in Valhalla

Locking it in

Howl at the full moon

Time to eat some food

Think something sweet;   I wish you would

Because you can't eat me

Negus, I'm sour D

Speaking on me is like drinking a bowl of
Buckley's

For anybody saying they sick,

The remedy, eye give them the whole clip
and cure it like an antibiotic

While Hell's population goes up and down like hydraulics

Eye drop this out of the sky, killing they pride

Words murder them slowly; watch my enemies die

Because negus lie, but numbers don't

Hov ain't lie, eye testify

Do the math like a mathematician

God works in mysterious ways, don't ask why

Cowards front, get shot, then ask GOD why

Because life wasn't a game... That's why

PRISON INDUSTRIAL COMPLEX

Sitting upstate,

Uncle Sam closed the gate

Where the C.O.'s are racist and breed the hate

Cowards go to the mess hall to eat and get ate

Make no mistake

This is no place for weakness

You better be living every word you speaking

The wolves will test you, G

For no reason

I'm waiting for shorty to come see me this
weekend

She bringing the haze and ten razors for the beef

So I can buff and sneak in

First Negus front gonna be leaking

I'm not cutting his face for fame

Things changed

My first aim is for the lame's jugular vein

Just to let the whole prison know I'm not playing

Even if I go to the box, I go out with a bang!

My prison nation! Do what you got to do but know you got to win

Try to find a way to make it out the pen

Negus coming out worse off then they went in, trying to find a way to make it out the pen

Size 9 and a half, try doing my time and a half

Upstate New York with the long shank in the stash

Razor fights on sight; try not to get slashed

Jail politics, you better learn them fast

Playing the bunk? Nah, I ain't a punk. I'm
connected to dog

Soon as eye walk through doors

See the wolves from my hood, I'm going to
howl out y'all

They ready to enforce any shots I call

Fresh out the box, they sent me to a new spot, fresh start

A new hub with new thuggs

I heard papi say moreno got it locked, and they call it the dog pound on D-Block

The C.0.'s try to control but never know what's about to happen under their nose

They shouldn't of let me back in population because I'm the shot caller that keeps the prison shaking

Funny how eye smoked more weed than I did in the street

Just so I can sleep and take my mind off the street

Even the warden be scared when it's tension in the air

You can come in and never get out of here

I'm in the yard on the bar, hitting it hard

In the middle of a war with Latin Kings and GODS

His cousin got cut, now the Crips involved

If blood get on a dog,

Damus going to jump off and Muslims praying that it all get squashed

NAKED

I'm in the mood for love

Simply because you're near me

My wand gets so hard when you stare at me

Tonight I'ma make the neighbors hear me

Your face is flawless, and that ass is phat

Negus can't wait to get back so I can hit that

Like soon as we get to my place

Let's get naked

No procrastination

Straight to the basics

You said you can't take it, horny & can't shake it

DEME got the good love, girl, you about to taste it

Swallow me whole. Oh! Don't waste it

Neo and Trinity making love in the Matrix, Cybersex

Bumping and grinding to the bass kicks

Sweating so much salt water, she starts to taste it

Saying my name

And I'm climaxing the Egyptian Goddess Nut
while she say it

Her fantasy is us

Laying here Naked

NO FOOD

When my mother gave birth,

They considered it a blessing eye was born second

Between me and my brethren

In a world where men make babies and keep it stepping

Couldn't understand it, seeing my mom stressing

With a single parent, what I witnessed I was
affected and she seen it in me

The angel and the demon in me

Look in my eyes, look in my eyes

You can see the blacktop on the ghetto
blocks where the hard rocks post up

Yup, to get that guap

Just for one shot at the American dream

But when the metal pop, they learn to lean
and rock

We all become products of what we seen a
lot

To the little boys and girls who dream a lot

I used to dream about things I wanted and
never got

That's why I speak with slang and walk with
a bop

Because that's where I grew up hard, as one
of the have-nots

Mommy in the bedroom crying

There isn't a lot of food in the fridge and my stomach still growling so slow

And his eyes are so cold, so cold

So now Mommy in the bedroom crying

Ain't got a lot of trust left; see every man lying, so now she know,

That when I grow up, there won't be a lot of love left inside me

Mama crying, Poppa lying

He was a Tyrant

Caught up in the streets, shot by the fire hydrant

All eye seen was violence

Eye was raised to be the violence

So I feed the violence like a beast that lay silent

A shooter's secret how real I keep it

Eye hate to brag, so ask the OG's on the ave

And they will tell you, "The little kid was bad."

Crack had my dad, PS 398

Thuggin' in my class, sucka punch a kid

Teacher asked, "Why are you so mad?"

Daddy strung out, so MaMa whip my ass

So all I know is whip a boy's ass

Lock, load and explode up and snatch they
cash

I'm from where boys are forced to grow up
fast

Shoot first, talk last; that's the lesson

I'm giving my mama they money, but now
their mother's stressing

GOLD MIND

The only place success comes before work is in the dictionary

The way you behave is hereditary

The way she throw the ass at me is kind of scary

She got that snapback Boomerang, Halle Berry

She see the cherry Mulsanne

And know I'm doing things, if I buy her a bag

Better believe she earned it

What her EX used to do, I'm not concerned with

I just want a friend to burn with, so don't ask for it

Because you gonna have to bust it open and dance for it

See all this money; if you want it, you can get it, girl

Come get it, come get it

And eye pick you to help me spend it like you winning, girl

So start digging, baby, because you messing with a gold mind

This is the era everybody is superficial

When you getting money, it's the broke negus to diss you

The issue, anybody could buy bottles

When every gangsta's a rapper and every stripper a model

She taking them ass shots, he downing them glass shots

They both fake it to make it, being the have-nots

Nah, I'm not hatin'

Eye just call it how eye see it, negus

They say speak the truth but I just want to be it

Stockholm Syndrome and you cant even see it

For them gold diggers with that shovel and that cake

That bubble and no waist, eye got bank just like Chase

Baby girl so pretty, and she takes it all in the face

But she don't mind because she know she got a gold mind

They call her bougie because she like them
Superstars

She wants to live like the kings and queens
we are

She likes fast cars, Aventador the meanest

Two different worlds; I'm from Mars, and
she's from Venus

She wants expensive things

Pink diamonds to its zenith but all eye got is black bottles

And hard penis

The God's a genius, always two steps ahead of her

Escalator, etc., etc.

TYPE OF TIME

Ah EE LA HA ILL ALLAH! Eye hope I take 10 of them before eye die

Heart full of hate, I can see it in their eyes

They don't want to see me dripping, they don't want to see me living

Driving this foreign car, living like a star

Getting chased by the women like I'm a GOD

They want the drip to end, but I'm harder than the cook on the stove

Once you go Black, you won't go back

That fire through the wire had them coming
in droves

Conscious Trap, 95 South

What type of time are you on? Hold on time
out

We on the type of time to kill a hundred
negus in a rhyme

On a track, and none of them Black

We going to ride, we on that type of time

The Moors from the N9ne is on that type of time

If the KKK wants it? We on that type of time

Neo-Nazis want to get it? We on that type of time

Protecting our hood, we on that type of time

We gon' ride because we on that type of time

This ain't Black-on-Black crime, killing your own kind

Because we no longer on that type of time

Blicky on deck, Mo

Ya dun know! Sankofa Shango

I'm going to blow, get the bag, and buy guns and ammo

'Cause when they come, there won't be nowhere to run

Black-on-Black crime, I'm not on that type
of time

Don't make me show you what type of time
I'm on

Don't get it trill, if eye have to eye will

But I rather have the little bros chill

And save those bullets for the skinheads up
the hill

Shoot a Black, Shoot a white

Does it matter? In self-defense of my people, it does

Blood or Cuz, feel this; it's all love

All my Moors in the Feds, hold your head

When you come home I got a Fez and some bread

Talking about you want to stop the violence in Hip Hop

First, you have to stop the violence by the cops

I SHOULD OF KNOWN

I would've took a Straight Stuntin model and a bottle of Hypnotic

For every click that played sick and I squeezed on

Every chick I G'd and wiped N.U.T.'s on

Girl, please excuse me; I'm slicing through

Lyrical Sean Michaels pied-piping you

Eye thank GOD for vaginas and brawlic diamonds

Look at you now; you could've been shining

What was all the drama for?

Eye was loving you more

Should've known you was slore, the way you wore that Christian Dior

Walk was mean

Thought you was on my team

But I thought wrong though,

Word born, Yo!

Played myself, admitted in this poem though

I invested in us like Bloomberg, New York

Your love worth so much I could bid you off

And get my money back, bet that

But the sign on your ass says no refunds,
and I regret that

REAL NEGUS

It's lit! We turnt up!

Who wants what? Haters want war, but they can't keep up

Real negus do what they want; they do what they can

We everywhere they aren't

In and out of state

They never leave the hood like D. Jordan in the paint

Outside the box, he don't got no shot

While I'm somewhere hot with a rich bad THOT

DEMEGOD.com, my life don't stop

Cough up a lung. Where you from? Murdaville, sun

Ain't nothing nice but the wheels

Spider, low grill

Eye got build powers on chill

Looking for rappers and dope boys to devour

We can build and destroy and break bread with the dirty Desert Eagle

Pop one in the head

Throw brick and start chopping negus

Get it how we live. We can knock the projects down and rebuild them as pyramids

The industry going to make room for the goons

Because this the era of the fuckboys and the coons

BLACK PANTHER

I'm a corporate thug banging like Shaka Zulu

Dress like Russell Simmons

Shirt read "Free Mutulu."

Thinking to myself, *what would Noble Drew do*?

787 vibrating on 11

My vibranium chain swing that circle seven

And they wonder why these devils can't kill me

Islam, to all my Sufis in Philly

Zkirs and ten trilly

Riding through the city, bumping Meek Milly

Deme like Marcus Garvey, living financial freedom

A team of corporate women are my business bodyguards

Thighs and hips and they all have bodies like they strip

Or they can catch a body on the strip

In the boardroom, Umi secures the bag

Word to the father, I'm conscious, but I'm
still a monster

The Black Panther and every ghetto's
Wakanda

Where the walking dead wander and wander

SHE LIKE RAPPERS

Poppin' so many bottles

She won't remember tomorrow

Because she gave me the ass, she asks for money to borrow

She see the cars and the crib

Know eye got it to give, but I ain't mad at her; she just trying to live

I'm not giving her shit

Adam gave Eve a rib so she want a rich man to give her a kid

But it won't be me; she know I'm a G

She like the rappers, ball players, and actors

She don't have too many choices, either them or the trappers

A black girl lost, and I'm her GPS

I'm going to show her that heaven is up under that sundress, yes!

NEGUS 2 GOD

We the GODS! But niggaz they used to call
us

Now we calling each real negus on every
corner

How can you fault us?

In the ghetto living so thoughtless

Having them big dreams of Bentleys,
Benzes, and Porsches

We metamorphosis into something
awesome, enormous

Lazy negus stay broke, but not the son of
Dolores

Gold crosses flossing in Porsches 400 horses

Body of a lion with the head of Horus

Kiss the game goodbye. I'm about to have it in a frenzy

GOD meant me to push a Bentley

Me and Mario Falcon taking' WAPS home

Strippers you can't afford, they all call me the Lord

High-end Tom Ford

Swallowing swords

Baby girl from Sweden, trick-or-treating

The sweetest kiss

New Edition, my Candy Girl. Eye eat her like Swedish Fish

Fist full of money and still charge it to the card

A negus turn, GOD

RAP/HIP HOP EXORCISM

Hip Hop forever, my lady, please don't cry

Here comes your knight in shining armor, ready to die

The gleam of the Maserati lights blinding the eyes

They blinded to the ways of the Most High

Cast out the demons that come to my shows

A thousand deaths to whoever killed Little MO

In North Carolina and eye swear on your mama

We better not find you

Set that ass on fire, bullets biting like hot piranhas

So powerful with just my words; I bring the
drama

Hand my little soldiers assault rifles and
Bibles, then let them choose

I guarantee they serve justice on the
evening news

So tell me, how the hell can we lose?

It's ours!

POLYGYNY

I got G5 dreams, me & my whole team

Living like kings, I'm the lord of the rings

I got five wives like a Sunni in Dubai

Falcon sex in the sky

Every one of them is fly

Häagen-Dazs, different flavors

In college with different majors

I teach them how to shoot, WNBA players

I ball with them and take them all out to
Vegas

This thing of ours, we never mind the haters

I tell them all there is no favorite

I just feast on their legs, and they tell me
I'm the greatest

Gold diggers want to eat?

Please beat your feet

I have more problems than I can handle; I
don't need to cheat

Want to be the next wife?

You have to get voted in

Either rolling in a Benz or rolling in a bucket

We gonna get this money and dare a
mutherfucka to touch it

Throw it back on me, girl

The GOD gonna love it

FRENEMIES

Music, pussy, and money got negus acting funny

Hate me or love me in the booth, I get it ugly

Fuckboy mad because his little THOT love me

I got nothing but love, dough, like one of my hitters, Bugsy

I rather give my goonies something to live
for

But they rather I give them something to die
for and ride for

Catch a homicide for

But I wouldn't waste my shooters' lives on
none of y'all

Kill them with kindness, offer these negus a
job

Bullets cost money, so broke negus aren't
worth it

I can just send a missile at them while they
watch the stripper twerking

If you're not in it to get it, then what's your
purpose?

I got love for my enemies

Yeah, I got love for them

But negus want to see the end of me

Until I get it, now them negus say they some kin to me

I got love, I got love for my enemies

Yeah, I got love for them

They don't want to see me pull up, so I pull up like what! What! What!

All the Treesha's trying to get to me when I pull up

Dirty Diana trying to get to me when I pull up

My negus deep, we like 15 when I pull up

Pull up, pull up! Pull up, pull up!

They want to see me pull up, so I pull up

Just to see a hater mad

I be loving that, so I go around the block twice and double back

Don't make me pop the trunk, you don't want none of that

WE DON'T

I don't kill negus no more, I kill racism

I don't diss Black women no more, I diss sexism

Sexual advances from men?

No, captain, I'm Gucci

Let me do me with all these women, bro; I'm Gucci!

I don't kill dealers no more, I kill the rat-ters

The dope boys that don't give back to the hood, I kill their trappers

I don't go to war no more, I do magic

I wave the gun and call on the demon, abracadabra!

We don't kill innocent kids or bystanders

They learn to aim from video games and real hammers

We don't kill people no more, just white extremist

Trump tried to label my family Black extremist

But we not Black; we Pan-African extremist

Black is a color, not a race or a creed

Everything African you want to delete it

The only thing we need to kill is our own demons

That's why these ignorant negus killing for no reason

ROLE MODEL

Hey, kids, don't you want to be just like me?

Get money like me and push the new V

Don't you want to be like the hottest rapper they are playing?

Don't you want to listen to every word that he saying?

Well guess what? Rap music is just entertainment

Like Van Damme kicking somebody face in

But a real Gangsta's life nothing to play with

I bang for all the realest G'z that never made it

BK made me, Mount Vernon, N.Y. raised me

My name was Danger, a BIG warning

Don't try to play me

I don't want to do you dirty, so don't make me

I'm the GOD with compassion, but don't mistake me for weak